This belongs to

Renee

Date

31 July 2013

Developed for busy moms, this journal has just enough room to capture five years' worth of memories and highlights for every day of the year. Each page has a quote or Bible verse for a touch of inspiration and lines at the bottom for your daily insights, descriptions, or memorable moments.

With a mom's busy schedule, there is not always time for long journal entries. Yet there is always time for a line or two.

Start any time. Write the year in the space provided. Jot down a sentence, blessing, or prayer. It is as easy as that. In five years you'll create a treasury of moments to be cherished for a lifetime.

January 1

*Line by line, moment by moment, special times
are etched into our memories in the permanent
ink of everlasting love in our relationships!*
Gloria Gaither

20___

20___

20___

20___

20___

January 2

$\mathcal{F}$ather, help me to take the time to create
stories with my children. May good memories
hold the generations together. Amen.
Scott Walker

20___

20___

20___

20___

20___

January 3

Put your hope in the LORD now and forever.
Psalm 131:3 NCV

20___

20___

20___

20___

20___

January 4

After the love of God, a mother's affection
is the greatest treasure here below.

20___

20___

20___

20___

20___

January 5

For whatever life holds for you and your family
in the coming days, weave the unfailing fabric
of God's Word through your heart and mind.
It will hold strong, even if the rest of life unravels.
Gigi Graham Tchividjian

20___

20___

20___

20___

20___

January 6

Then Jesus took the children in his arms,
put his hands on them, and blessed them.
Mark 10:16 NCV

20___

20___

20___

20___

20___

January 7

*When you are dealing with a child,
keep all your wits about you and sit on the floor.*
A. O'Malley

20__

20__

20__

20__

20__

January 8

Where your pleasure is, there is your treasure;
where your treasure, there your heart;
where your heart, there your happiness.
Augustine

20___

20___

20___

20___

20___

January 9

We plan the way we want to live,
but only GOD makes us able to live it.
Proverbs 16:9 MSG

20__

20__

20__

20__

20__

January 10

The influence of a mother in the lives of
her children is beyond calculation.
James E. Faust

20__

20__

20__

20__

20__

January 11

There is no other closeness in human life like
the closeness between a mother and her baby—
chronologically, physically, and spiritually they are just
a few heartbeats away from being the same person.
Susan Chever

20___

20___

20___

20___

20___

January 12

Mother had a thousand thoughts to get through within a day, and...most of these were about avoiding disaster.
Natalie Kusz

20___

20___

20___

20___

20___

January 13

What a wonderful God we have—
he is...the source of every mercy, and the one who
so wonderfully comforts and strengthens us.
2 Corinthians 1:3-4 TLB

20___

20___

20___

20___

20___

January 14

This is the most extraordinary thing about motherhood—
finding a piece of yourself separate and apart
that all the same you could not live without.
Jodi Picoult

20___

20___

20___

20___

20___

January 15

God specializes in things fresh and firsthand. His plans for you this year may outshine those of the past.... He's preparing to fill your days with reasons to give Him praise.
Joni Eareckson Tada

20___

20___

20___

20___

20___

January 16

Facing a mirror you see merely your own countenance; facing your child you finally understand how everyone else has seen you.
Daniel Raeburn

20__

20__

20__

20__

20__

January 17

Embrace this God-life. Really embrace it, and nothing
will be too much for you.... Pray for absolutely everything,
ranging from small to large. Include everything as you
embrace this God-life, and you'll get God's everything.
Mark 11:22–24 MSG

20___

20___

20___

20___

20___

January 18

Kind words can be short and easy to speak,
but their echoes are truly endless.
Mother Teresa

20___

20___

20___

20___

20___

January 19

*Cleaning your house while your kids are still growing
is like shoveling the walk before it stops snowing.*
Phyllis Diller

20__

20__

20__

20__

20__

January 20

All mothers are rich when they love their children....
Their love is always the most beautiful of joys.
Maurice Maeterlinck

20__

20__

20__

20__

20__

January 21

*He surrounds me with loving-kindness
and tender mercies. He fills my life with good
things! My youth is renewed like the eagle's!*
Psalm 103:4–5 TLB

20___

20___

20___

20___

20___

January 22

If you have a special need today, focus your full attention on the goodness and greatness of your Father rather than on the size of your need. Your need is so small compared to His ability to meet it.

20__

20__

20__

20__

20__

January 23

When you look at your life, the greatest
happinesses are family happinesses.
Joyce Brothers

20___

20___

20___

20___

20___

January 24

Children are a great comfort in your old age.
And they help you reach it sooner too.
M. Lionel Kauffman

20__

20__

20__

20__

20__

January 25

For GOD is sheer beauty, all-generous
in love, loyal always and ever.
Psalm 100:5 MSG

20___

20___

20___

20___

20___

January 26

We must not, in trying to think about how we can make a big difference, ignore the small daily differences we can make which, over time, add up to big differences that we often cannot foresee.
Marian Wright Edelman

20___

20___

20___

20___

20___

January 27

I have found the best way to give advice to your children
is to find out what they want and then advise them to do it.
Harry S. Truman

20__

20__

20__

20__

20__

January 28

You are a holy people, who belong to the Lord your God. Of all the people on earth, the Lord your God has chosen you to be his own special treasure.
Deuteronomy 7:6 NLT

20__

20__

20__

20__

20__

January 29

A good laugh is sunshine in a house.
William Makepeace Thackeray

20__

20__

20__

20__

20__

January 30

Motherhood: If it was going to be easy, it never
would have started with something called labor.
Barbara Johnson

20___

20___

20___

20___

20___

January 31

If your children spend most of their time
in other people's houses, you're lucky; if they all
congregate at your house, you're blessed.
Mignon McLaughlin

20___

20___

20___

20___

20___

February 1

The heart of the giver makes the gift dear and precious.
Martin Luther

20___

20___

20___

20___

20___

February 2

Serve the Lord enthusiastically. Rejoice in our
confident hope. Be patient in trouble, and keep
on praying. When God's people are in need, be ready
to help them. Always be eager to practice hospitality.
Romans 12:11-13 NLT

20__

20__

20__

20__

20__

February 3

*A mother is not a person to lean upon,
but a person to make leaning unnecessary.*
Dorothy Canfield Fisher

20___

_____

_____

_____

20___

_____

_____

_____

20___

_____

_____

_____

20___

_____

_____

_____

20___

_____

_____

_____

February 4

*If evolution really works, how come
mothers only have two hands?*
Milton Berle

20___

20___

20___

20___

20___

February 5

Once we discover how to appreciate the timeless values
in our daily experiences, we can enjoy the best things in life.
Harry Hepner

20__

20__

20__

20__

20__

February 6

*Most of all, love each other as if your life depended
on it. Love makes up for practically anything.*
1 Peter 4:8 MSG

20___

20___

20___

20___

20___

February 7

Children are comforted when they're held in their parents' arms. Hugs help sparkle up a day.
Gary Smalley & John Trent

20___

20___

20___

20___

20___

February 8

Before you go to bed, write down three "gratefuls" for the
day and three "did wells" (they can even include something
as simple as doing the laundry)—the results can be amazing!
Carol Burnett

20__

20__

20__

20__

20__

February 9

Half the joy of life is in little things taken on the run.
Let us run if we must—even the sands do that—
but let us keep our hearts young and our eyes open
that nothing worth our while shall escape us.
Victor Cherbuliez

20__

20__

20__

20__

20__

February 10

*E*verything we know about God's Word is summed
up in a single sentence: Love others as you love
yourself. That's an act of true freedom.
Galatians 5:14 MSG

20___

20___

20___

20___

20___

February 11

Children are unpredictable. You never know what inconsistency they're going to catch you in next.
Franklin P. Jones

20___

20___

20___

20___

20___

February 12

Where we love is home, home that our feet may leave, but not our hearts.
Oliver Wendell Holmes

20__

20__

20__

20__

20__

February 13

Be kind to each other, tenderhearted, forgiving
one other, just as God has forgiven you.
Ephesians 4:32 TLB

20__

20__

20__

20__

20__

February 14

There is an enduring tenderness in the love of a mother...
that transcends all other affections of the heart.
Washington Irving

20__

20__

20__

20__

20__

February 15

Children help us rediscover the joy, excitement, and mystery of the world we live in.

20___

20___

20___

20___

20___

February 16

When we recall the past, we usually find that
it is the simplest things—not the great occasions—
that in retrospect give off the greatest glow of happiness.
Bob Hope

20___

20___

20___

20___

20___

February 17

If you...know how to give good gifts to your
children, how much more will your heavenly Father
give the Holy Spirit to those who ask him.
Luke 11:13 NLT

20__

20__

20__

20__

20__

February 18

What guides us is children's response, their joy
in learning to dance, to sing, to live together.
It should be a guide to the whole world.
Yehudi Menuhin

20___

20___

20___

20___

20___

February 19

If you have three or four—or more—chickabiddies,
you're dancing on a hot griddle all the time.
You don't have time to think about anything else.
Sharon Creech

20__

20__

20__

20__

20__

February 20

The God who created, names, and numbers the stars
in the heavens also numbers the hairs of my head....
He pays attention to very big things and to very small ones.
What matters to me matters to Him, and that changes my life.
Elisabeth Elliot

20___

20___

20___

20___

20___

February 21

If you puff yourself up, you'll get the wind knocked out of you. But if you're content to simply be yourself, your life will count for plenty.
Matthew 23:11–12 MSG

20___

20___

20___

20___

20___

February 22

What is home? It is the laugh of a baby, the song
of a mother, the strength of a father, warmth of loving hearts,
lights from happy eyes, kindness, loyalty, companionship.

20___

20___

20___

20___

20___

February 23

The most important thing she'd learned over
the years was that there was no way to be a perfect
mother and a million ways to be a good one.
Jill Churchill

20___

20___

20___

20___

20___

February 24

How we spend our days is, of course,
how we spend our lives.
Annie Dillard

20__

20__

20__

20__

20__

February 25

Don't worry about anything; instead, pray about everything;
tell God your needs, and don't forget to thank him for his
answers. If you do this, you will experience God's peace, which
is far more wonderful than the human mind can understand.
Philippians 4:6-7 TLB

20__

20__

20__

20__

20__

February 26

*Human beings are the only creatures
that allow their children to come back home.*
Bill Cosby

20___

20___

20___

20___

20___

February 27

One hundred years from now, it will not matter what
my bank account was, how big my house was, or what kind
of car I drove. But the world may be a little better,
because I was important in the life of a child.
Forest Witcraft

20___

20___

20___

20___

20___

February 28

Each day is a gift. The days come together to make the pieces of our God-created lives a beautiful whole.
Bonnie Jensen

20___

20___

20___

20___

20___

February 29

*D*on't you see that children are GOD's best gift?
the fruit of the womb his generous legacy?
Psalm 127:3 MSG

20__

20__

20__

20__

20__

March 1

*A mother's arms are made of tenderness
and children sleep soundly in them.*
Victor Hugo

20___

20___

20___

20___

20___

March 2

Grown-ups never understand anything for themselves, and it is tiresome for children to be always and forever explaining things to them.
Antoine de Saint-Exupéry

20__

20__

20__

20__

20__

March 3

Encouragement is being a good listener, being positive, letting others know you accept them for who they are. It is offering hope, caring about the feelings of another, understanding.
Gigi Graham Tchividjian

20___

20___

20___

20___

20___

March 4

Because the Lord is my Shepherd,
I have everything I need!
He lets me rest in the meadow grass
and leads me beside the quiet streams.
Psalm 23:1–2 TLB

20___

20___

20___

20___

20___

March 5

There are many little ways to enlarge your child's
world. Love of books is the best of all.
Jacqueline Kennedy Onassis

20__

20__

20__

20__

20__

March 6

The highest calling in this world is to
be a good and loving parent.

20__

20__

20__

20__

20__

March 7

*If we take care of the moments, the years
will take care of themselves.*
Maria Edgeworth

20__

20__

20__

20__

20__

March 8

*R*egardless of what else you put on, wear love. It's your
basic, all-purpose garment. Never be without it.
Colossians 3:14 MSG

20__

20__

20__

20__

20__

March 9

The only time a woman wishes she were a year
older is when she is carrying a baby.
M. Marsh

20__

20__

20__

20__

20__

March 10

*Each day of our lives we make deposits in
the memory banks of our children.*
Charles R. Swindoll

20__ ....
....
....

20__ ....
....
....

20__ ....
....
....

20__ ....
....
....

20__ ....
....
....

March 11

Kids are like sponges: They absorb all your
strength and leave you limp. But give 'em
a squeeze and you get it all back.
Barbara Johnson

20__

20__

20__

20__

20__

March 12

God can do anything, you know—far more than you could ever
imagine or guess or request in your wildest dreams! He does it...
by working within us, His Spirit deeply and gently within us.
Ephesians 3:20–21 MSG

20__

20__

20__

20__

20__

March 13

Family life is too intimate to be preserved
by the spirit of justice. It can be sustained
by a spirit of love which goes beyond justice.
Reinhold Niebuhr

20__

20__

20__

20__

20__

March 14

Pajama-clad tot calling out to family: "I'm going upstairs to say my prayers now. Anyone want anything?"

20__

20__

20__

20__

20__

March 15

Love has been called the most effective motivational force in all the world. When love is at work in us, it is remarkable how giving and forgiving, understanding and tolerant we can be.

Charles Swindoll

20___

20___

20___

20___

20___

March 16

Whatever is true, whatever is noble, whatever is right, whatever
is pure, whatever is lovely, whatever is admirable—if anything
is excellent or praiseworthy—think about such things.
Philippians 4:8 NIV

20___

20___

20___

20___

20___

March 17

I wish you love and strength and faith and wisdom,
Goods, gold enough to help some needy one.
I wish you songs, but also blessed silence,
And God's sweet peace when every day is done.
Dorothy Nell McDonald

20__

20__

20__

20__

20__

March 18

May you wake each day with God's blessings
and sleep each night in His keeping. And as you grow
older, may you always walk in His tender care.
Irish Blessing

20__

20__

20__

20__

20__

March 19

The very word "motherhood" has an emotional
depth and significance few terms have. It bespeaks
nourishment and safety and sheltering arms.
Marjorie Holmes

20__

20__

20__

20__

20__

March 20

Be content with who you are, and don't put on airs. God's
strong hand is on you; he'll promote you at the right time.
Live carefree before God; he is most careful with you.
1 Peter 5:6–7 MSG

20__

20__

20__

20__

20__

March 21

You know that children are growing up when they start asking questions that have answers.
John J. Plomp

20__

20__

20__

20__

20__

March 22

Creating a family in this turbulent world is an act
of faith, a wager that against all odds there will be a future,
that love can last, that the heart can triumph against all
adversities and even against the grinding wheel of time.
Dean Koontz

20__

20__

20__

20__

20__

March 23

[Do not] forget the obvious, the little joys, the meals
together, the birthday celebrations, the weeping
together in time of pain, the wonder of the sunset,
or the daffodil peeping through the snow.
Madeleine L'Engle

20__

20__

20__

20__

20__

March 24

*Y*ou should be like one big happy family,
full of sympathy toward each other, loving one
another with tender hearts and humble minds.
1 Peter 3:8 TLB

20__

20__

20__

20__

20__

March 25

The truth is, most of our alleged superheroes make meals,
make beds, make ends meet, make mistakes,
make amends, make love, make up, and mostly make do.
Marianne E. Neifert

20__

20__

20__

20__

20__

March 26

Supermom wasn't a bad job description.
The pay was lousy if you were talking about real money.
But the payoff was priceless in so many other ways.
Roxanne Henke

20___

20___

20___

20___

20___

March 27

Love is extravagant in the price it is willing to pay, the time it is willing to give...and the strength it is willing to spend.
Joni Eareckson Tada

20__

20__

20__

20__

20__

March 28

*I love the LORD because he hears my voice
and my prayer for mercy.
Because he bends down to listen,
I will pray as long as I have breath!*
Psalm 116:1-2 NLT

20___

20___

20___

20___

20___

March 29

Give a little love to a child and you get a great deal back.
John Ruskin

20__

20__

20__

20__

20__

March 30

*Easter is the demonstration of God that life
is essentially spiritual and timeless.*
Charles M. Crow

20__

20__

20__

20__

20__

March 31

*H*ome. A place where when you get there,
you know your heart has been there all along.
Gloria Gaither

20___

20___

20___

20___

20___

April 1

May the Lord continually bless you with heaven's blessings as well as with human joys.
Psalm 128:5 TLB

20__

20__

20__

20__

20__

April 2

*Most of us become parents long before
we have stopped being children.*
Mignon McLaughlin

20__

20__

20__

20__

20__

April 3

I think of the garden after the rain;
And hope to my heart comes singing,
"At morn the cherry-blooms will be white,
And the Easter bells be ringing!"
Edna Dean Procter

20__

20__

20__

20__

20__

April 4

*Home is the most popular, and will be the most
enduring of all earthly establishments.*
Channing Pollock

20__

20__

20__

20__

20__

April 5

*I will not forget you. See, I have inscribed
you on the palms of my hands.*
Isaiah 49:15-16 NRSV

20__

20__

20__

20__

20__

April 6

The only thing worth stealing is a kiss from a sleeping child.
Joe Houldsworth

20__

20__

20__

20__

20__

April 7

Home is first school and first church for young ones, where they learn what is right, what is good, and what is kind, where they go for comfort when they are hurt or sick; where joy is shared and sorrow eased.... That is home. God bless it!

20___

20___

20___

20___

20___

April 8

The quickest way for a parent to get a child's
attention is to sit down and look comfortable.
Lane Olinghouse

20___

20___

20___

20___

20___

April 9

*Those who bring sunshine to the lives
of others cannot keep it from themselves.*
Sir James M. Barrie

20__

20__

20__

20__

20__

April 10

I call on you, my God, for you will answer me;
turn your ear to me and hear my prayer.
Psalm 17:6 NIV

20___

20___

20___

20___

20___

April 11

When God thought of mother, He must have laughed
with satisfaction—so rich, so deep, so divine, so full
of soul, power, and beauty, was the conception!
Henry Ward Beecher

20__

20__

20__

20__

20__

April 12

It is a special gift to be able to view
the world through the eyes of a child.

20__

20__

20__

20__

20__

April 13

Having someone who understands is a great
blessing for ourselves. Being someone who
understands is a great blessing to others.
Janette Oke

20__

20__

20__

20__

20__

April 14

*E*mbracing what God does for you
is the best thing you can do for him.
Romans 12:1 MSG

20___

20___

20___

20___

20___

April 15

You may have tangible wealth untold;
Caskets of jewels and coffers of gold.
Richer than I you can never be—
I had a mother who read to me.
Strickland Gillilan

20__

20__

20__

20__

20__

April 16

You will always be your child's favorite toy.
Vicki Lansky

20___

20___

20___

20___

20___

April 17

*L*ift up your eyes. Your heavenly Father waits
to bless you—in inconceivable ways to make your
life what you never dreamed it could be.
Anne Ortlund

20___

20___

20___

20___

20___

April 18

You make known to me the path of life;
you will fill me with joy in your presence,
with eternal pleasures at your right hand.
Psalm 16:11 NIV

20___

20___

20___

20___

20___

April 19

What we are teaches the child far more
than what we say, so we must be what we
want our children to become.
Joseph Chilton Pearce

20__

20__

20__

20__

20__

April 20

Have you any idea how many children it takes to turn off one light in the kitchen? Three. It takes one to say *What light?* and two more to say *I didn't turn it on.*
Erma Bombeck

20__

20__

20__

20__

20__

April 21

*Love is an act of endless forgiveness,
a tender look which becomes a habit.*
Peter Ustinov

20__

20__

20__

20__

20__

April 22

Yes, you have been with me from birth;
from my mother's womb you have cared for me.
No wonder I am always praising you!
Psalm 71:6 NLT

20___

20___

20___

20___

20___

April 23

There was a place in childhood that I remember well,
And there a voice of sweetest tone bright fairy tales did tell.
Samuel Lover

20___

20___

20___

20___

20___

April 24

A mother is a mother from the moment her baby
is first placed in her arms until eternity.
Sarah Strohmeyer

20___

20___

20___

20___

20___

April 25

Stay on good terms with each other, held together by love.
Hebrews 13:1 MSG

20__

20__

20__

20__

20__

April 26

When our relationships are born in the heart of God,
they bring out the best in us, for they are nurtured by love.
Don Lessin

20__

20__

20__

20__

20__

April 27

*This delicious home-feeling is one
of the choicest gifts a parent can bestow.*
Isabella Mary Mayson

20__

20__

20__

20__

20__

April 28

The mighty mystery of motherhood is this:
How is it that doing it all feels
like nothing is ever getting done?
Rebecca Woolf

20__

20__

20__

20__

20__

April 29

All I want is for you to be able to develop a way
of life in which you can spend plenty of time together
with the Master without a lot of distractions.
1 Corinthians 7:35 MSG

20__

20__

20__

20__

20__

April 30

Only He who created the wonders
of the world entwines hearts in an eternal way.

20__

20__

20__

20__

20__

May 1

*God...help me to be faithful so my children
will learn faith.
Help me to love so that my children
will be loving.*
Marian Wright Edelman

20___

20___

20___

20___

20___

May 2

Call it clan, call it a network, call it a tribe, call it a family.
Whatever you call it, whoever you are, you need one.
Jane Howard

20___

20___

20___

20___

20___

May 3

*May the Lord be loyal to you in return
and reward you with his unfailing love!*
2 Samuel 2:6 NLT

20___

20___

20___

20___

20___

May 4

Any child can tell you that the sole purpose of a middle
name is so he can tell when he's really in trouble.
Dennis Fakes

20__

20__

20__

20__

20__

May 5

Mother love is the fuel that enables a normal
human being to do the impossible.
Marion C. Garretty

20__

20__

20__

20__

20__

May 6

Love is the true means by which the world is enjoyed:
our love to others, and others' love to us.
Thomas Traherne

20__

20__

20__

20__

20__

May 7

As parents feel for their children,
GOD feels for those who fear Him.
Psalm 103:13 MSG

20__

20__

20__

20__

20__

May 8

In spite of the six thousand manuals on child raising
in the bookstores, child raising is still a dark continent
and no one really knows anything. You just need
a lot of love and luck—and, of course, courage.
Bill Cosby

20__

20__

20__

20__

20__

May 9

*If we are cheerful and contented, all nature smiles...
the flowers are more fragrant, the birds sing more
sweetly, and the sun, moon, and stars all appear
more beautiful and seem to rejoice with us.*
Orison Swett Marden

20__

20__

20__

20__

20__

May 10

On Mother's Day, I think moms should be able to wake
up and say to themselves: I'm a domestic goddess!
Barbara Johnson

20__

20__

20__

20__

20__

May 11

God's blessing makes life rich;
nothing we do can improve on God.
Proverbs 10:22 MSG

20__

20__

20__

20__

20__

May 12

Families give us many things—love and meaning, purpose and an opportunity to give, and a sense of humor.

20___

_____

_____

_____

20___

_____

_____

_____

20___

_____

_____

_____

20___

_____

_____

_____

20___

_____

_____

_____

May 13

Somehow, when the going gets rough
and our protective covering is stripped away, close,
tender moments come about more freely.
Jere Kessler Corven

20__

20__

20__

20__

20__

May 14

*R*emember that you are needed.
There is at least one important work to be done
that will not be done unless you do it.
Charles Allen

20__

20__

20__

20__

20__

May 15

In him our hearts rejoice,
for we trust in his holy name.
Psalm 33:21 NIV

20___

20___

20___

20___

20___

May 16

I still think the prayer without words is the best....
When the golden moments come, when God enables one really
to pray without words, who but a fool would reject the gift?
C. S. Lewis

20__

20__

20__

20__

20__

May 17

Sometimes the laughter in mothering
is the recognition of the ironies and absurdities.
Sometime, though, it's just pure, unthinking delight.
Barbara Schapiro

20__

20__

20__

20__

20__

May 18

£ife is not intended to be simply a round of work,
no matter how interesting and important that work may be.
A moment's pause to watch the glory
of a sunrise or a sunset is soul satisfying, while a bird's
song will set the steps to music all day long.
Laura Ingalls Wilder

20___

20___

20___

20___

20___

May 19

May the LORD cause you to flourish,
both you and your children.
May you be blessed by the LORD,
the Maker of heaven and earth.
Psalm 115:14–15 NIV

20__

20__

20__

20__

20__

May 20

If you want your children to improve, let them overhear the nice things you say about them to others.
Haim G. Ginott

20___

20___

20___

20___

20___

May 21

Raising kids is part joy and part guerilla warfare.
Ed Asner

20__

20__

20__

20__

20__

May 22

To a child, a home is a place where you come in out of the rain. A shelter from the wind. A place where love lives.

20__

20__

20__

20__

20__

May 23

Where your treasure is, there your heart will be also.
Matthew 6:21 NIV

20__

20__

20__

20__

20__

May 24

I think, at a child's birth, if a mother could ask
a fairy godmother to endow it with the most
useful gift, that gift should be curiosity.
Eleanor Roosevelt

20__

20__

20__

20__

20__

May 25

*L*ove is that condition in which the happiness
of another person is essential to your own.
Robert Heinlein

20__

20__

20__

20__

20__

May 26

A mother is a person who seeing there are only four pieces of pie for five people, promptly announces she never did care for pie.
Tenneva Jordan

20__

20__

20__

20__

20__

May 27

The eternal God is your refuge,
and underneath are the everlasting arms.
Deuteronomy 33:27 TLB

20__

20__

20__

20__

20__

May 28

*God bless my mother; all that I am
or ever hope to be I owe to her.*
Abraham Lincoln

20__

20__

20__

20__

20__

May 29

No one ever outgrows the need for a mother's love.
Janette Oke

20__

20__

20__

20__

20__

May 30

*Tradition gives us a sense of solidarity and roots,
a knowing there are some things one can count on.*
Gloria Gaither

20___

20___

20___

20___

20___

May 31

God is our refuge and strength,
an ever-present help in trouble.
Therefore we will not fear.
Psalm 46:1–2 NIV

20___

20___

20___

20___

20___

June 1

A mother is the truest friend we have, when trials, heavy
and sudden, fall upon us; when adversity takes the place
of prosperity...still will she cling to us, and endeavor...to dissipate
the clouds of darkness, and cause peace to return to our hearts.
Washington Irving

20__

20__

20__

20__

20__

June 2

When we do the best that we can, we never know what miracle is wrought in our life, or in the life of another.
Helen Keller

20___

20___

20___

20___

20___

June 3

Be generous with the different things God gave you,
passing them around so all get in on it: if words, let it be
God's words; if help, let it be God's hearty help. That way,
God's bright presence will be evident in everything.
1 Peter 4:10–11 MSG

20___

20___

20___

20___

20___

June 4

Happy moments—those moments when you feel fully alive—certainly exist. They swim by us every day like shining, silver fish waiting to be caught.
Alice Steinback

20__

20__

20__

20__

20__

June 5

God takes care of His own. He knows our needs.
He anticipates our crises. He is moved by our weaknesses....
And at just the right moment He steps
in and proves Himself as our faithful heavenly Father.
Charles Swindoll

20__

20__

20__

20__

20__

June 6

*Perhaps this moment is unclear, but let it be—
even if the next, and many moments after that, are unclear,
let them be. Trust that God will help you work them out.*
Wendy Moore

20___

20___

20___

20___

20___

June 7

*In my desperation I prayed, and the LORD
listened; he saved me from all my troubles.*
Psalm 34:6 NLT

20__

20__

20__

20__

20__

June 8

Few gifts in life will last as long or touch the heart as deeply
As the very special gift of family.
Craig S. Tunks

20___

20___

20___

20___

20___

June 9

*Time is the coin of your life. It is the only coin you
have, and only you can determine how it will be spent.
Be careful lest you let other people spend it for you.*
Carl Sandburg

20___

20___

20___

20___

20___

June 10

A happy life is not built up of tours abroad and pleasant holidays, but of little clumps of violets noticed by the roadside.
Edward Wilson

20__

20__

20__

20__

20__

June 11

May the LORD bless you and protect you.
May the LORD smile on you and be gracious to you.
May the LORD show you his favor and give you his peace.
Numbers 6:24–26 NLT

20__

20__

20__

20__

20__

June 12

Prayer isn't about words.... It's about trust—trust that God understands what we need and how we feel.
Maria Massei-Rosato

20__

20__

20__

20__

20__

June 13

For a mother is the only person on earth
Who can divide her love among ten children
And each child still has all her love.

20__

20__

20__

20__

20__

June 14

Slow down awhile! Push aside the press
of the immediate. Take time today, if only for a moment,
to lovingly encourage each one in your family.
Gary Smalley & John Trent

20___

20___

20___

20___

20___

June 15

The LORD will guide you always; he will satisfy your needs
in a sun-scorched land.... You will be like a
well-watered garden, like a spring whose waters never fail.
Isaiah 58:11 NIV

20__

20__

20__

20__

20__

June 16

*P*atience asks us to live the moment to the fullest, to be
completely present to the moment, to taste the here and now,
to be where we are…. Let's be patient and trust that the treasure
we look for is hidden in the ground on which we stand.
Henri J. M. Nouwen

20___

20___

20___

20___

20___

June 17

Fill the cup of happiness for others, and there will be enough overflowing to fill yours to the brim.
Rose Pastor Stokes

20__

20__

20__

20__

20__

June 18

An aware parent loves all children he
or she meets and interacts with—for you are
a caretaker for those moments in time.
Doc Childre

20__

20__

20__

20__

20__

June 19

*Regarding life together and getting along with each other...
you're God-taught in these matters. Just love one another!*
1 Thessalonians 4:9 MSG

20___

20___

20___

20___

20___

June 20

It doesn't take monumental feats to make the world a better place. It can be as simple as letting someone go ahead of you in a grocery line.
Barbara Johnson

20__

20__

20__

20__

20__

June 21

Motherhood...is the only love I have known that is expansive and that could have stretched to contain with equal passion more than one object.
Erma Kurtz

20___

20___

20___

20___

20___

June 22

These are the children God has given me.
God has been good to me.
Genesis 33:5 NCV

20___

20___

20___

20___

20___

June 23

*A woman who is full of tender mercy and a soft
vulnerability is a powerful, lovely woman.*
John and Stasi Eldridge

20__

20__

20__

20__

20__

June 24

*If a child is to keep his inborn sense of wonder...
he needs the companionship of at least one adult
who can share it, rediscovering with him the joy,
excitement, and mystery of the world we live in.*
Rachel Carson

20___

20___

20___

20___

20___

June 25

Mothers are lots of things—doctors, writers, lawyers,
gardeners, actresses, cooks, police officers, sometimes
even truck drivers. And mothers. Thank You, Lord.
Madeleine L'Engle

20__

20__

20__

20__

20__

June 26

He will once again fill your mouth with
laughter and your lips with shouts of joy.
Job 8:21 NLT

20__

20__

20__

20__

20__

June 27

A good laugh is as good as a prayer sometimes.
Lucy Maud Montgomery

20__

20__

20__

20__

20__

June 28

We can change the world inside our own houses.
Take the gift of this moment and make something
beautiful of it. Few worthwhile experiences just
happen; memories are made on purpose.
Gloria Gaither

20__

20__

20__

20__

20__

June 29

Feeling grateful or appreciative of someone or something in your life actually attracts more of the things that you appreciate and value into your life. And the more of your life that you like and appreciate, the healthier you'll be.
Christiane Northrup

20__

20__

20__

20__

20__

June 30

If we want our children to pray, they must hear us pray.
Quin Sherrer

20__

20__

20__

20__

20__

July 1

A cheerful heart is good medicine.
Proverbs 17:22 NIV

20__

20__

20__

20__

20__

July 2

The gift of praise is the best gift you can
give your child, any time of the year.

20__ ....
....
....

20__ ....
....
....

20__ ....
....
....

20__ ....
....
....

20__ ....
....
....

July 3

The incredible gift of the ordinary! Glory comes
streaming from the table of daily life.
Macrina Wiederkehr

20___

20___

20___

20___

20___

July 4

*The mother is the most precious possession of the nation,
so precious that society advances its highest
well-being when it protects the functions of the mother.*
Ellen Key

20___

20___

20___

20___

20___

July 5

See how great a love the Father has bestowed on us,
that we would be called children of God; and such we are.
1 John 3:1 NASB

20__

20__

20__

20__

20__

July 6

What parent can tell when some fragmentary gift
of knowledge or wisdom will enrich her children's lives?
Or how a small seed of information passed from one generation
to another may generate a new science, a new industry.
Helena Rubinstein

20___

20___

20___

20___

20___

July 7

The world is full of riches, but none of them can compare
with the treasures that lie within a mother's heart.
Patricia H. Rushford

20___

20___

20___

20___

20___

July 8

*You have no strength but what God gives,
and you have all of the strength that God can give.*
Andrew Murray

20___

20___

20___

20___

20___

July 9

It's impossible to make another person feel good without doing the same to ourselves.
Hal Urban

20___

20___

20___

20___

20___

July 10

For the LORD grants wisdom!
From his mouth come knowledge and understanding.
He grants a treasure of common sense to the honest.
He is a shield to those who walk with integrity.
Proverbs 2:6–7 NLT

20__

20__

20__

20__

20__

July 11

Go with the flow, but pray God keeps you afloat.
Angela Martinez

20___

20___

20___

20___

20___

July 12

My precious family and friends have taught me that joy and sorrows, storms and sunshine, tears and laughter are all part of living—and the sun does shine on the other side.
Margaret Jensen

20___

20___

20___

20___

20___

July 13

The measure of your real success
is one you cannot spend—
it's the way your child describes you
when talking to a friend.
Martin Buxbaum

20___

20___

20___

20___

20___

July 14

Beauty is not generic. Quite often, the thing that makes you memorable is the thing that makes you different.
Laura Mercier

20__

20__

20__

20__

20__

July 15

*Love has its source in God, for love
is the very essence of His being.*
Kay Arthur

20___

20___

20___

20___

20___

July 16

Sometimes our light goes out but is blown again into flame by
an encounter with another human being. Each of us owes
the deepest thanks to those who have rekindled this inner light.
Barbara Glanz

20__

20__

20__

20__

20__

July 17

*Character is what emerges from all the little things
you were too busy to do yesterday, but did anyway.*
Mignon McLaughlin

20__

20__

20__

20__

20__

July 18

My child, never forget the things I have taught you.
Store my commands in your heart.
If you do this, you will live many years,
and your life will be satisfying.
Proverbs 3:1-2 NLT

20___

20___

20___

20___

20___

July 19

*More things are wrought by prayer
Than this world dreams of.*
Alfred, Lord Tennyson

20___

20___

20___

20___

20___

July 20

*M*oments spent listening, talking, playing, and sharing
together may be the most important times of all.
Gloria Gaither

20__

20__

20__

20__

20__

July 21

In the happy moments, praise God.
In the difficult moments, seek God. In the quiet
moments, trust God. In every moment, thank God.
Robert Albert Wood

20__

20__

20__

20__

20__

July 22

Your heavenly Father knows your needs. He will always
give you all you need from day to day.... It gives your
Father great happiness to give you the Kingdom.
Luke 12:30-32 TLB

20__

20__

20__

20__

20__

July 23

The family is the first setting in which socialization takes place and where children learn to live with mutual respect for one another. A family is where a child learns to display affection, control his temper, and pick up his toys.

Marianne E. Neifert

20___

20___

20___

20___

20___

July 24

God has a purpose for your life and no
one else can take your place.

20__

20__

20__

20__

20__

July 25

Youth fades; love droops, the leaves of friendship fall;
A mother's secret hope outlives them all.
Oliver Wendell Holmes

20___

20___

20___

20___

20___

July 26

Celebrate God all day, every day. I mean, revel in him!
Philippians 4:4 MSG

20__

20__

20__

20__

20__

July 27

The one thing children wear out faster than shoes is parents.
John J. Plomp

20__

20__

20__

20__

20__

July 28

An infinite God can give all of Himself to each of His children. He does not distribute Himself that each may have a part, but to each one He gives all of Himself.
A. W. Tozer

20___

20___

20___

20___

20___

July 29

*The wind rushing through the grass, the thrush
in the treetops, and children tumbling in senseless
mirth stir in us a bright faith in life.*
Donald C. Peattie

20__

20__

20__

20__

20__

July 30

Every good and perfect gift is from above, coming down
from the Father of the heavenly lights,
who does not change like shifting shadows.
James 1:17 NIV

20__

20__

20__

20__

20__

July 31

The informality of family life is a blessed condition
that allows us to become our best while looking our worst.
Marge Kennedy

20___

20___

20___

20___

20___

August 1

*Growth comes when we aim for our ideal,
and not necessarily when we achieve it.*
Sheryl Towers

20__

20__

20__

20__

20__

August 2

A mother's love is the heart of the home. Her children's sense of security and self-worth are found there.

20__

20__

20__

20__

20__

August 3

Being the God you are...please, just one more thing:
Bless my family; keep your eye on them always.
2 Samuel 7:28 MSG

20___

20___

20___

20___

20___

August 4

Make a memory with your children,
Take the time in busy days;
Have some fun while they are growing,
Show your love in gentle ways.
Elaine Hardt

20___

20___

20___

20___

20___

August 5

God's heart is the most sensitive and tender of all.
No act goes unnoticed, no matter how insignificant or small.
Richard Foster

20__

20__

20__

20__

20__

August 6

Thank goodness for August—the time to lie back and wallow in the knowledge that there is absolutely no occasion to rise to.
Barbara Johnson

20___

20___

20___

20___

20___

August 7

*N*ever let loyalty and kindness leave you!...
Write them deep within your heart.
Then you will find favor with both God and people,
and you will earn a good reputation.
Proverbs 3:3-4 NLT

20___

20___

20___

20___

20___

August 8

A four-year-old prayed, "And forgive us our trash baskets as we forgive those who put trash in our baskets."

20___

20___

20___

20___

20___

August 9

When things go wrong, as they sometimes will,
When the road you're trudging seems all uphill...
When care is pressing you down a bit,
Rest, if you must—but don't you quit!

20___

20___

20___

20___

20___

August 10

God invented parenthood. He is for us. He is for each
of our children. He is champion of their lives, their years,
their health, their calling, and their eternal destiny.
Ralph T. Mattson and Thom Black

20__

20__

20__

20__

20__

August 11

Follow the way of love.
1 Corinthians 14:1 NIV

20___

20___

20___

20___

20___

August 12

*Before I was a mom
I didn't know the feeling of having my heart outside my body....
I didn't know that something so small
Could make me feel so important.*

20___

20___

20___

20___

20___

August 13

I am beginning to learn that it is the sweet, simple
things of life which are the real ones after all.
Laura Ingalls Wilder

20___

20___

20___

20___

20___

August 14

It's a simple solution...you change one thing, and suddenly you've changed everything.
Rebecca Onie

20__

20__

20__

20__

20__

August 15

My God is changeless in His love for me,
and He will come and help me.
Psalm 59:10 TLB

20___

20___

20___

20___

20___

August 16

Family faces are magic mirrors. Looking at people who belong to us, we see the past, present, and future.
Gail Lumet Buckley

20__

20__

20__

20__

20__

August 17

Thank You, Father, for the beautiful surprises You are planning
for me today. So often in my life...an unexpected burst
of golden sunshine has exploded through a black cloud, sending
inspiring shafts of warm, beautiful sunshine into my life.
Robert Schuller

20___

20___

20___

20___

20___

August 18

When you have laboriously accomplished your
daily task, go to sleep in peace. God is awake.
Victor Hugo

20__

20__

20__

20__

20__

August 19

*Parents are not interested in justice;
they are interested in quiet.*
Bill Cosby

20___

20___

20___

20___

20___

August 20

One thing I have asked from the LORD, that I shall seek:
That I may dwell in the house of the LORD, all the
days of my life, To behold the beauty of the LORD.
Psalm 27:4-5 NASB

20___

20___

20___

20___

20___

August 21

I believe the way to get out of bed is with a leap and to hold the conviction that each day is going to be the greatest day of my life.
Sidney Harman

20___

20___

20___

20___

20___

August 22

They might not need me; but they might.
I'll let my head be just in sight;
A smile as small as mine might be
Precisely their necessity.
Emily Dickinson

20__

20__

20__

20__

20__

August 23

The hardest part of raising a child is teaching them to ride bicycles. A shaky child on a bicycle for the first time needs both support and freedom. The realization that this is what the child will always need can hit hard.
Sloan Wilson

20__

20__

20__

20__

20__

August 24

She is clothed with strength and dignity;
she can laugh at the days to come.
Proverbs 31:25 NIV

20___

20___

20___

20___

20___

September 4

Guard your heart above all else,
for it determines the course of your life.
Proverbs 4:23 NLT

20__

20__

20__

20__

20__

September 5

*Love each other as God loves you,
with an intense and particular love.*
Mother Teresa

20__

20__

20__

20__

20__

September 6

Half our life is spent trying to find
something to do with the time we have
rushed through life trying to save.
Will Rogers

20___

20___

20___

20___

20___

September 7

*Try to see the beauty "in your own backyard,"
to notice the miracles of everyday life, to see
the specialness of your own children.*
Gloria Gaither

20___

20___

20___

20___

20___

September 8

Your Father knows what you need before you ask Him.
Matthew 6:8 NIV

20__

20__

20__

20__

20__

September 9

A wonderful mother, a special friend, that's what you've been to me...so much a part of lovely times I keep in memory.

20___

20___

20___

20___

20___

September 10

*I love these little people; and it is not a slight thing
when they, who are so fresh from God, love us.*
Charles Dickens

20__

20__

20__

20__

20__

September 11

I will comfort you as a mother comforts her child.
Isaiah 66:13 NCV

20__

20__

20__

20__

20__

September 12

There is no need to plead that the love of God shall
fill our hearts as though He were unwilling to fill us....
Love is pressing around us on all sides like air. Cease
to resist it and instantly love takes possession.
Amy Carmichael

20___

20___

20___

20___

20___

September 13

Being a full-time mother is one of the highest salaried
jobs in my field, since the payment is pure love.
Mildred B. Vermont

20__

20__

20__

20__

20__

September 14

Enthusiasm is a divine possession.
Margaret E. Sangster

20___

20___

20___

20___

20___

September 15

I am giving you a new commandment: Love each other. Just as I have loved you, you should love each other.
John 13:34 NLT

20___

20___

20___

20___

20___

September 16

Who ran to help me when I fell,
And would some pretty story tell,
Or kiss the place to make it well?
My mother.
Ann Taylor Gilbert

20__

20__

20__

20__

20__

September 17

What families have in common the world around is that they are the place where people learn who they are and how to be that way.
Jean Illsley Clarke

20__

20__

20__

20__

20__

September 18

There is a time for risky love. There is a time for extravagant gestures. There is a time to pour out your affections on one you love. And when the time comes—seize it, don't miss it.
Max Lucado

20__

20__

20__

20__

20__

September 19

This is the day which the LORD has made;
Let us rejoice and be glad in it.
Psalm 118:24 NASB

20___

20___

20___

20___

20___

September 20

When we call on God, He bends down His ear to listen,
as a father bends down to listen to his little child.
Elizabeth Charles

20__

20__

20__

20__

20__

September 21

The ultimate goal of parenthood is to allow your children
to become the persons God intended them to be.

20___

20___

20___

20___

20___

September 22

Laughter is a shock absorber.
Phil Callaway

20___

20___

20___

20___

20___

September 23

The Kingdom of God is not a matter of what we eat
or drink, but of living a life of goodness and peace and joy.
Romans 14:17 NLT

20___

20___

20___

20___

20___

September 24

As a child my family's menu consisted
of two choices: take it, or leave it.
Buddy Hackett

20__

20__

20__

20__

20__

September 25

*Nothing is so strong as gentleness,
and nothing so gentle as real strength.*
François de Sales

20___

20___

20___

20___

20___

September 26

I looked on child rearing not only as a work of love and duty but as a profession that was fully as interesting and challenging as any honorable profession in the world and one that demanded the best that I could bring to it.
Rose Fitzgerald Kennedy

20__

20__

20__

20__

20__

September 27

*Take your everyday, ordinary life—your sleeping,
eating, going-to-work, and walking-around life—
and place it before God as an offering.*
Romans 12:1 MSG

20__

20__

20__

20__

20__

September 28

Self-sacrifice is often necessary. But if you work yourself to ashes, there is nothing left with which to ignite the rest of your life.
Linda Hawes Clever

20___

20___

20___

20___

20___

September 29

Grant me the power of saying things too
simple and too sweet for words.
Coventry Patmore

20__

20__

20__

20__

20__

September 30

What feeling is so nice as a child's hand in yours?
So small, so soft and warm, like a kitten
huddling in the shelter of your clasp.
Marjorie Holmes

20__

20__

20__

20__

20__

October 1

God has surely listened and has heard my prayer.
Praise be to God, who has not rejected my
prayer or withheld his love from me!
Psalm 66:19-20 NIV

20___
_____
_____
_____

20___
_____
_____
_____

20___
_____
_____
_____

20___
_____
_____
_____

20___
_____
_____
_____

October 2

How many hopes and fears, how many ardent wishes
and anxious apprehensions are twisted together
in the threads that connect the parent with the child!
Samuel Griswold Goodrich

20___

20___

20___

20___

20___

October 3

There is nothing more thrilling in this world,
I think, than having a child that is yours,
and yet is mysteriously a stranger.
Agatha Christie

20___

20___

20___

20___

20___

October 4

*I long to accomplish a great and noble task,
but it is my chief duty to accomplish humble
tasks as though they were great and noble.*
Helen Keller

20__

20__

20__

20__

20__

October 5

*You're not in this alone. I want you woven into a tapestry
of love, in touch with everything there is to know of God.*
Colossians 2:1-2 MSG

20__

20__

20__

20__

20__

October 6

A mother is...one who can take the place of all others, but whose place no one else can take.
Gaspard Mermillod

20___

20___

20___

20___

20___

October 7

[It's] 24/7. Once you sign on to be a mother,
that's the only shift they offer.
Jodi Picoult

20__

20__

20__

20__

20__

October 8

God has a thousand ways
Where I can see not one;
When all my means have reached their end
Then His have just begun.
Esther Guyot

20__

20__

20__

20__

20__

October 9

I know what it is to be in need, and I know what
it is to have plenty. I have learned the secret
of being content in any and every situation.... I can do
everything through Him who gives me strength.
Philippians 4:12–13 NIV

20___

20___

20___

20___

20___

October 10

*The heritage of children is timeless.
Our children are our messages to the future.*
Billy Graham

20___

20___

20___

20___

20___

October 11

Stories first heard at a mother's knee are never wholly
forgotten—a little spring that never quite dries up.
Giovanni Domenico Ruffini

20__

20__

20__

20__

20__

October 12

To love by freely giving is its own reward.
To be possessed by love and to in turn give love
away is to find the secret of abundant life.
Gloria Gaither

20__

20__

20__

20__

20__

October 13

The Lord your God is with you....
He will take great delight in you,
He will quiet you with his love,
He will rejoice over you with singing.
Zephaniah 3:17 NIV

20__

20__

20__

20__

20__

October 14

Any kid will run any errand for you if you ask at bedtime.
Red Skelton

20__

20__

20__

20__

20__

October 15

A young child, a fresh, uncluttered mind, the world
before him—to what treasures will you lead him?
Gladys M. Hunt

20___

20___

20___

20___

20___

October 16

To live in prayer together is to walk in love together.
Margaret Moore Jacobs

20___

20___

20___

20___

20___

October 17

Pay close attention...to what your father tells you; never forget what you learned at your mother's knee. Wear their counsel like flowers in your hair, like rings on your fingers.
Proverbs 1:8–9 MSG

20__

20__

20__

20__

20__

October 18

A family is a perpetual source of encouragement,
advocacy, assurance, and emotional refueling that
empowers a child to venture with confidence into
the greater world and to become all that he can be.
Marianne E. Neifert

20__

20__

20__

20__

20__

October 19

If it weren't for the last minute, nothing would get done.

20___

20___

20___

20___

20___

October 20

Usually parents who are lucky in the kind of children they have, have children who are lucky in the kind of parents they have.

20___

20___

20___

20___

20___

October 21

Those who hope in the LORD will renew their strength.
They will soar on wings like eagles;
they will run and not grow weary,
they will walk and not faint.
Isaiah 40:31 NIV

20__

20__

20__

20__

20__

October 22

The secret of life is that all we have
and are is a gift of grace to be shared.
Lloyd John Ogilvie

20___

20___

20___

20___

20___

October 23

I always wondered why babies spend so much time sucking their thumbs. Then I tasted baby food.
Robert Orben

20__

20__

20__

20__

20__

October 24

God's timing is rarely our timing.... He numbers our days
and knows our moments and our hours. Our task is to trust.
Os Guinness

20___

20___

20___

20___

20___

October 25

Charm is deceptive, and beauty does not last;
but a woman who fears the LORD will be greatly praised.
Proverbs 31:30 NLT

20__

20__

20__

20__

20__

October 26

We are not called by God to do extraordinary things,
but to do ordinary things with extraordinary love.
Jean Vanier

20__

20__

20__

20__

20__

October 27

*The loveliest masterpiece of the heart
of God is the heart of a mother.*
Thérèse of Lisieux

20___

20___

20___

20___

20___

October 28

You're a foundation builder.... What could be more important than helping to shape and mold others' lives?
Guy Doud

20___

20___

20___

20___

20___

October 29

But this I call to mind, and therefore I have hope: The steadfast
love of the LORD never ceases, his mercies never come
to an end; they are new every morning; great is your faithfulness.
Lamentations 3:21-23 NRSV

20___

20___

20___

20___

20___

October 30

To speak gratitude is courteous and pleasant, to enact gratitude
is generous and noble, but to live gratitude is to touch heaven.
Johannes A. Gaertner

20__

20__

20__

20__

20__

October 31

A happy life is...one long continuous chain of little joys,
little whispers from the spiritual world,
and little gleams of sunshine on our daily work.
Edward Wilson

20__

20__

20__

20__

20__

November 1

A mother understands what a child does not say.
Jewish Proverb

20___

20___

20___

20___

20___

November 2

*Love each other with genuine affection,
and take delight in honoring each other.*
Romans 12:10 NLT

20__

20__

20__

20__

20__

November 3

*Happiness comes of the capacity to feel deeply,
to enjoy simply, to think freely, to risk life, to be needed.*
Storm Jameson

20__

20__

20__

20__

20__

November 4

Nothing can match the treasure of common
memories, of trials endured together, of quarrels
and reconciliations and generous emotions.
Antoine de Saint-Exupéry

20__

20__

20__

20__

20__

November 5

Be on the lookout for mercies. The more we
look for them, the more of them we will see.
Blessings brighten when we count them.
Maltbie D. Babcock

20___

20___

20___

20___

20___

November 6

*May the God of hope fill you with all joy and peace
as you trust in him, so that you may overflow with hope.*
Romans 15:13 NIV

20___

20___

20___

20___

20___

November 7

There's nothing that can help you understand your beliefs
more than trying to explain them to an inquisitive child.
Frank A. Clark

20___

20___

20___

20___

20___

November 8

*The joy of motherhood: What a woman experiences
when all the children are finally in bed.*
Barbara Johnson

20__

20__

20__

20__

20__

November 9

We have been in God's thought from all eternity,
and in His creative love, His attention never leaves us.
Michael Quoist

20__

20__

20__

20__

20__

November 10

*Trust in the LORD with all your heart;
do not depend on your own understanding.
Seek his will in all you do,
and he will show you which path to take.*
Proverbs 3:5-6 NLT

20___

20___

20___

20___

20___

November 11

*If there be one thing pure...that can endure,
when all else passes away...it is a mother's love.*
Marchioness de Spadara

20___

20___

20___

20___

20___

November 12

*My hope for my children must be that they respond
to the still, small voice of God in their own hearts.*
Andrew Young Jr.

20__

20__

20__

20__

20__

November 13

Getting things accomplished isn't nearly as important as taking time for love.
Janette Oke

20__

20__

20__

20__

20__

November 14

Start children off on the way they should go,
and even when they are old they will not turn from it.
Proverbs 22:6 NIV

20__

20__

20__

20__

20__

November 15

*God pardons like a mother who kisses
the offense into everlasting forgetfulness.*
Henry Ward Beecher

20___

20___

20___

20___

20___

November 16

Courage doesn't always roar. Sometimes courage is the little voice at the end of the day that says...I'll try again tomorrow.

20___

20___

20___

20___

20___

November 17

Sweater: garment worn by child when its mother is feeling chilly.
Ambrose Bierce

20__

20__

20__

20__

20__

November 18

Love...puts up with anything,
Trusts God always,
Always looks for the best....
Love never dies.
1 Corinthians 13:4, 8 MSG

20___

20___

20___

20___

20___

November 19

Blessed be childhood, which brings down something
of heaven into the midst of our rough earthliness.
Henri Frédéric Amiel

20__

20__

20__

20__

20__

November 20

A mother who walks with God knows He only asks her to take care of the possible and to trust Him with the impossible.
Ruth Bell Graham

20___

20___

20___

20___

20___

November 21

To be grateful is to recognize the love of God in everything
He has given us—and He has given us everything.
Thomas Merton

20__

20__

20__

20__

20__

November 22

I will pour out my Spirit on your descendants,
and my blessings on your children.
Isaiah 44:3 NLT

20__

20__

20__

20__

20__

November 23

Thanksgiving is a time of quiet reflection...an annual
reminder that God has, again, been ever so faithful.
The solid and simple things of life are brought into clear focus.
Charles Swindoll

20___

20___

20___

20___

20___

November 24

There are three ways to get something done: do it yourself, employ someone, or forbid your children to do it.
Monta H. Crane

20__

20__

20__

20__

20__

November 25

We never know the love of the parent until
we become parents ourselves.
Henry Ward Beecher

20__

20__

20__

20__

20__

November 26

Give thanks for everything to God the Father.
Ephesians 5:20 NLT

20___

20___

20___

20___

20___

November 27

A child enters your home and for the next twenty years makes so much noise you can hardly stand it. The child departs, leaving the house so silent you think you are going mad.
John Andrew Holmes

20__

20__

20__

20__

20__

November 28

*Gratitude is a twofold love—love coming to visit us,
and love running out to greet a welcome guest.*
Henry Van Dyke

20__

20__

20__

20__

20__

November 29

Who takes a child by the hand takes a mother by the heart.
Danish Proverb

20___

20___

20___

20___

20___

November 30

The Lord says, "As surely as I live, your children
will be like jewels that a bride wears proudly."
Isaiah 49:18 NCV

20__

20__

20__

20__

20__

December 1

Thank God for dirty dishes;
They have a tale to tell.
While other folks go hungry,
We're eating pretty well.

20___

20___

20___

20___

20___

December 2

Affection is the most satisfying reward a child can receive. It costs nothing, is readily available, and provides great encouragement.

20___

20___

20___

20___

20___

December 3

$\mathcal{E}$ach day is a treasure box of gifts from God, just
waiting to be opened. Open your gifts with excitement.
You will find forgiveness attached to ribbons of joy.
You will find love wrapped in sparkling gems.
Joan Clayton

20__

20__

20__

20__

20__

December 4

I will lie down and sleep in peace, for you alone, O LORD, make me dwell in safety.
Psalm 4:8 NIV

20__

20__

20__

20__

20__

December 5

There's no greater gift at Christmas than to have everything you want, before you open presents.
Ann Marjorie

20___

20___

20___

20___

20___

December 6

*Celebration is more than a happy feeling.
Celebration is an experience. It is liking others,
accepting others, laughing with others.*
Douglas R. Stuva

20__

20__

20__

20__

20__

December 7

If God, like a father, denies us what we want now, it is in order to give us some far better thing later on. The will of God, we can rest assured, is invariably a better thing.
Elisabeth Elliot

20___

20___

20___

20___

20___

December 8

My beloved friends, let us continue to love each other
since love comes from God. Everyone who loves is born
of God and experiences a relationship with God.
1 John 4:7 MSG

20__

20__

20__

20__

20__

December 9

Spread love everywhere you go: first of all in your
own home. Give love to your children,
to a wife or husband, to a next-door neighbor.
Mother Teresa

20___

20___

20___

20___

20___

December 10

*Instant availability without continuous presence
is probably [the] best role a mother can play.*
L. Bailyn

20___

20___

20___

20___

20___

December 11

*May no gift be too small to give, nor too simple to receive,
which is wrapped in thoughtfulness and tied with love.*
L. O. Baird

20__

20__

20__

20__

20__

December 12

[Jesus] said to them, "Anyone who welcomes a little
child like this on my behalf welcomes me."
Mark 9:36–37 NLT

20___

20___

20___

20___

20___

December 13

It is good to be children sometimes, and never better than at Christmas, when its mighty Founder was a child Himself.
Charles Dickens

20__

20__

20__

20__

20__

December 14

In the midst of the shopping and the wrapping
and the arranging of presents under your tree this Christmas,
may you not forget the gifts you cannot yet hold in your hands.
T. D. Jakes

20___

20___

20___

20___

20___

December 15

God sends children to enlarge our hearts and to make us
unselfish and full of kindly sympathies and affections.
Mary Howitt

20___

20___

20___

20___

20___

December 16

Give generously, for your gifts will return to you later.
Ecclesiastes 11:1 TLB

20__

20__

20__

20__

20__

December 17

If there is love in your heart Christmas can last forever.
Marion Schoeberlein

20___

20___

20___

20___

20___

December 18

*Christmas waves a magic wand over this world,
and behold, everything is softer and more beautiful.*
Norman Vincent Peale

20__

20__

20__

20__

20__

December 19

*The virgin will be with child and will give birth to a son,
and they will call him Immanuel—which means, "God with us."*
Matthew 1:23 NIV

20___

20___

20___

20___

20___

December 20

Memories are treasures that we can enjoy again and again.

20__

20__

20__

20__

20__

December 21

Happiness is being at peace, being with loved ones, being comfortable.... But most of all, it's having those loved ones.
Johnny Cash

20___

20___

20___

20___

20___

December 22

The magical dust of Christmas glittered on the cheeks of humanity ever so briefly, reminding us of what is worth having and what we were intended to be.
Max Lucado

20___

20___

20___

20___

20___

December 23

The holidays are welcome to me partly because they are such rallying points for the affections, which get so much thrust aside in the business and preoccupations of daily life.
George E. Woodberry

20__

20__

20__

20__

20__

December 24

For to us a child is born, to us a son is given,
and the government will be on his shoulders. And
he will be called Wonderful Counselor, Mighty
God, Everlasting Father, Prince of Peace.
Isaiah 9:6 NIV

20__

20__

20__

20__

20__

December 25

The most vivid memories of Christmases past
are usually not of gifts given or received, but of
the spirit of love, the special warmth of Christmas
worship, the cherished little habits of the home.
Lois Rand

20__

20__

20__

20__

20__

December 26

Mother is the one we count on for the things that matter most of all.
Katharine Butler Hathaway

20__

20__

20__

20__

20__

December 27

Go out into the darkness and put your hand
into the hand of God. That shall be to you better
than light and safer than a known way.
Minnie Louise Haskins

20__   20__

20__   20__

20__   20__

20__   20__

20__   20__

Ellie Claire™ Gift & Paper Corp.
Brentwood, TN 37027
EllieClaire.com

Moments to Treasure: An Inspirational Five-Year Memory Book for Busy Moms
© 2013 by Ellie Claire Gift & Paper Corp.

ISBN 978-1-60936-760-2

Scripture references are from the following sources: The Holy Bible, New International
Version®, NIV®. Copyright © 1973, 1978, 1984, 2011 by Biblica, Inc.™ Used by permission of
Zondervan. All rights reserved worldwide. The New American Standard Bible® (NASB),
copyright © 1960, 1962, 1963, 1968, 1971, 1972, 1973, 1975, 1977, 1995 by The Lockman
Foundation. Used by permission. The New Revised Standard Version Bible (NRSV), copyright
1989, 1995, Division of Christian Education of the National Council of the Churches of Christ
in the United States of America. Used by permission. The Holy Bible, New Living Translation
(NLT), copyright 1996, 2004, 2007 by Tyndale House Foundation. Used by permission of
Tyndale House Publishers, Inc., Carol Stream, Illinois 60188. *The Message* (MSG) . Copyright
© 1993, 1994, 1995, 1996, 2000, 2001, 2002 by Eugene Peterson. Used by permission of
NavPress, Colorado Springs, CO. *The Living Bible* (TLB) © 1971. Used by permission of
Tyndale House Publishers, Inc., Carol Stream, Illinois 60188. The New Century Version®
(NCV). Copyright © 1987, 1988, 1991, 2005 by Thomas Nelson, Inc. Used by permission.
All rights reserved.

Excluding Scripture verses and deity pronouns, in some quotations references
to men and masculine pronouns have been replaced with gender-neutral
or feminine references. Additionally, in some quotations we have carefully
updated verb forms and wording that may distract modern readers.

Compiled by Marilyn Jansen
Cover and interior design by Studio Gearbox | studiogearbox.com

Ellie Claire Gift & Paper Corp. is an imprint of Worthy Publishing.

Printed in China